USBORNE FIRST READING
Level Three

USBORNE FIRST READING

The **Dinosaur**
Who Lost His **ROAR**

Russell Punter
Illustrated by Andy Elkerton

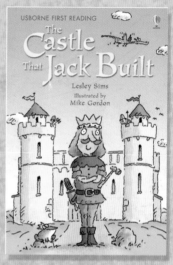

USBORNE FIRST READING

The **Castle**
That **Jack Built**

Lesley Sims

Illustrated by
Mike Gordon

USBORNE FIRST READING

**Chicken
Licken**

retold by
Russell Punter
Illustrated by Ann Kronheimer

USBORNE FIRST READING

The **Three Little
Pigs**

retold by
Susanna Davidson
Illustrated by Georgien Overwater

This is a story about

a dragon,

some villagers,

a salesman

and a gang of robbers.

Danny the dragon lived in some woods, beside a tiny village.

Some dragons are scary...

...but Danny was friendly.

Everyone in the village liked Danny.

And Danny liked
everyone in the village.

Each night, he visited every villager. He lit their fires.

He cooked their food.

He lit their candles as it grew dark.

Then he went home,
feeling happy.

One day, a stranger came
to the village.

"Roll up!" he cried.
"Buy Mr. Marvo's magic
fire sticks."

The villagers had
never seen magic fire
sticks before.

"What do they do?"
asked Joe.

"I'll show you," said
Mr. Marvo.

"They can light your fires
when you're cold."

"They can cook your food when you're hungry."

"And they can light your candles when it gets dark."

The villagers were amazed.

They bought all the magic
fire sticks on the wagon.

That night, Danny visited
the villagers as usual.

"Shall I light your fire?"
he asked Joe.

"I've got magic fire sticks," said Joe. "I don't need a dragon."

Danny walked to the
house next door.

"Shall I cook your food?"
he asked Peg.

"I've got magic fire
sticks," said Peg.
"I don't need a dragon."

25

Danny went to the
next house.

"Shall I light your candles?" he asked Sam.

"I've got magic fire
sticks," said Sam. "I don't
need a dragon."

It was the same story at
every house.

"No one needs me any
more," Danny thought.

He walked into the woods
and tried not to cry.

At that moment, a gang
of robbers was passing
the village.

They noticed the smoke of the fires.

They saw the light of the candles.

And they smelled the
food cooking.

"Grub's up!" cried the
chief robber.

The robbers stormed into the village.

They pushed the villagers away from their fires.

They snatched away
their food.

And they carried away
their candles.

"Who can help us?" cried
the villagers.

"Not me!" said Mr.
Marvo, and he ran away.

In the woods, Danny heard
the cries of the villagers.

He ran out of the woods
and into the village.

Danny charged up to
the robbers.

He set their beards
on fire...

toasted their feet...

and burned their bottoms.

The robbers ran off and
were never seen again.

The thankful villagers gave Danny his job back...

...and found another use for Mr. Marvo's magic sticks.

ZZZZZZZZZZZ

USBORNE FIRST READING
Level Four

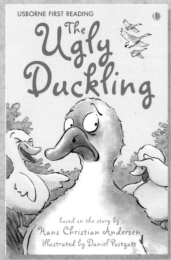

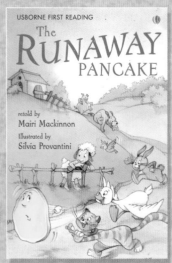